# TRACTORS

## James Nixon

**W**
FRANKLIN WATTS
LONDON•SYDNEY

An Appleseed Editions book

First published in 2010 by Franklin Watts
338 Euston Road, London NW1 3BH

Franklin Watts Australia
Hachette Children's Books
Level 17/207 Kent St, Sydney, NSW 2000

© 2010 Appleseed Editions

Created by Appleseed Editions Ltd,
Well House, Friars Hill, Guestling,
East Sussex TN35 4ET

Planning and production by Discovery Books Limited
Designed by D.R. ink
Cover design by Blink Media
Edited by James Nixon

ISBN: 978 1 4451 0032 6

Dewey Classification: 629.2'252

A CIP catalogue for this book is available from the British Library.

Photograph acknowledgements
Alamy Images: pp. 13 bottom (Peter Titmuss), 17 (Hans Miglbauer/WoodyStock), 19 top (Nigel Catlin); CASE: p.
7 top; Challenger/AGCO Corporation: pp. 5 bottom, 9, 18 top, 21 bottom, 23 bottom, 29 top; Classic Tractor
Magazine: p. 29 bottom (Rory Day); Getty Images: pp. 8 (Richard Drury), 24 (Mond Terakopian/AFP); John Deere:
pp. 7 bottom, 13 top, 28; Massey Ferguson/AGCO Corporation: pp. 5 middle, 6, 19 bottom, 20, 22, 23 top;
Musee de la Civilisation: p. 11 bottom; Shutterstock: pp. 4 (Mark William Richardson), 5 top (Alexey Buhantsov),
8 bottom (Marek Pawluczuk), 10 (M.D. Baker), 11 top (DCW Creations), 12, 14, 15 top (Niels Quist), 15 bottom
(Manfred Steinbach), 16 top (Niels Quist), 16 bottom (Phillip Minnis), 21 top (Dariusz Gora), 25 top (Graham
Taylor), 26 (Margo Harrison), 27 top (Neil Roy Johnson), 27 bottom (Michael Rubin); Wikimedia: p. 25 bottom
(Hayes Pulling).

Cover photos: Shutterstock: top; Massey Ferguson/AGCO Corporation: bottom.

Printed in China

Franklin Watts is a division of Hachette Children's Books,
www.hachette.co.uk

# Contents

# Tractors on the move

Tractors are great big, powerful machines. Most tractors work on farms. They can do all kinds of jobs. They pull trailers, lift loads and **plough** fields.

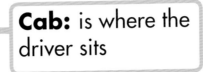

**Cab:** is where the driver sits

**Bonnet:** the tractor's engine is underneath

**Engine:** powers the tractor's wheels

**Counterweight:** balances the tractor when it is pulling heavy machinery

# Mighty machine

The Challenger MT975B is the world's most powerful tractor. Its massive engine pumps out over 600 horsepower!

# In the cab

Inside the cab, the driver uses many levers and switches to work the tractor's parts. The driver's seat is up high, so he or she can see all around.

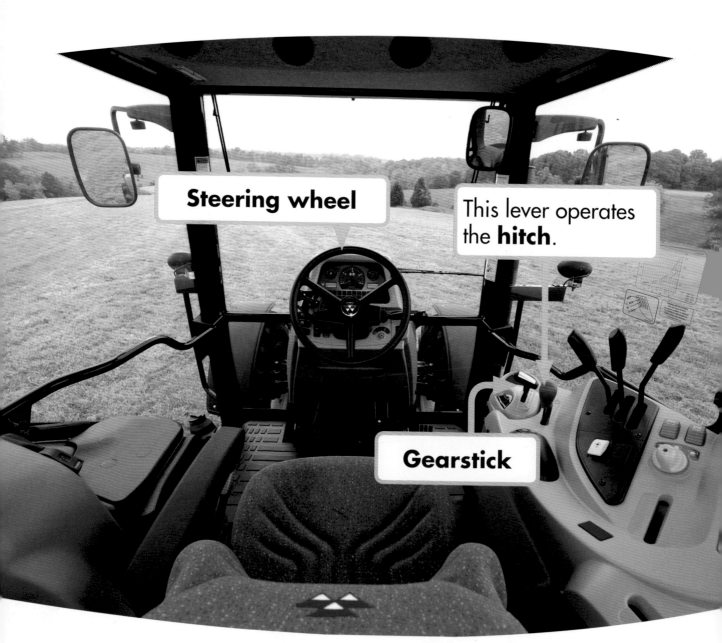

**Steering wheel**

This lever operates the **hitch**.

**Gearstick**

# Stop!

A tractor has two brake pedals. The left-hand pedal stops the back-left wheel and the right-hand pedal does the same on the right. The driver must press both at the same time to stop the tractor.

**Brake pedals**

## Spotlights

Tractor drivers often have to work through the night. Big spotlights help them find their way in the dark.

# Ploughing

A field needs ploughing before crops can be planted. Tractors pull a plough across the ground. The blades break up and turn the soil.

## The hitch

Ploughs are pulled using a hitch at the back of the tractor. The hitch hooks on to the plough or other machinery.

Hitch

**Harrows**

After ploughing the tractor pulls a set of **harrows**. This breaks the clumps of soil into even smaller bits. To finish, the tractor pulls a roller to flatten the land. Now it is ready for planting.

## Making tunnels

**The mole plough is a type of plough that makes tunnels deep in the ground. The tunnels are used for laying pipes.**

# Sowing seeds

Tractors pull big **seed drills** to plant seeds into the ground. A seed drill sows many rows of seeds at once.

Hopper

## Hopper

The seeds are stored in a container called a hopper (above). As the tractor moves along, the seeds are sucked out of the hopper. They travel down through tubes and into the ground.

**Hoppers**

Seed drills can have one large hopper or a row of smaller hoppers (above).

## Old ways

Before tractors were invented small seed drills were pushed by hand (right). Even longer ago, farmers just used their hands to scatter the seeds.

# Spraying crops

Once the seeds are planted, tractors are used to spray **fertilisers** and **weedkillers** on the crops. This helps the crops grow better.

## Long arms

Crop sprayers are huge bits of machinery. The arms reach out over 36 metres! The farmer doesn't have to drive over large parts of the field, which would damage the crop.

# Boom

The long arm is called the boom. The spray comes out of the boom through a row of nozzles.

**Nozzles**

**Boom**

The boom folds up so the tractor can travel on roads.

# ulling trailers

Farmers can hook trailers to the back of their tractors and carry large and heavy loads. Trailers transport things, such as potatoes, grain or bales of **hay**.

## Muck spreading

A muck spreader is a special type of trailer. Inside is a set of spinning paddles that throw **manure** out onto the ground. The manure adds goodness to the soil.

Spinning paddles

## Wheels

Tractors need huge wheels to travel over rough ground. The deep tread on the wheels grip the earth and stop the tractor slipping.

Tread

# Harvesters

When the crops are fully grown it is time to **harvest**. Many crops are gathered by a **combine harvester** and emptied into a trailer.

## Picking grapes

In **vineyards** special tractors are used to harvest the grapes. The tractor's shape means it can drive over the top of the vines. As it moves, the grapes are knocked off into a large bin.

# Out of the earth

Tractors can harvest some crops with a machine attached to the back.

Big harvesting machines (below) can pull up many rows of **root vegetables**, such as potatoes, all in one go.

# Grass cutters

Tractors mow large fields of grass by pulling wide cutting blades. The grass is then bundled up as animal feed or left to dry out to turn into hay.

## Power take-off

The tractor provides power to the machinery that it pulls. A **shaft** transfers the engine's power to the machine. This is called the power take-off.

Power take-off

Farmers use cutting equipment to keep their land neat and tidy, too. This tractor has a hedge trimmer attached.

## Mini-tractors

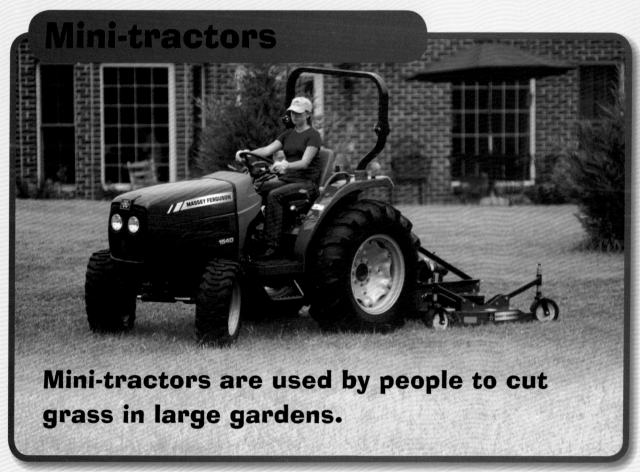

**Mini-tractors are used by people to cut grass in large gardens.**

# Balers

Once grass is cut, a tractor pulls a machine called a haybob over it. This flicks the grass into neat rows.

Haybob

When the rows of grass have dried out, a baling machine is driven over them. It picks up the hay as it goes. Inside the baler, the hay is rolled up with rubber belts into the shape of a cylinder and dropped out of the back.

Straw is baled up in the same way. Some balers pack straw and hay into brick shapes.

## Lifting bales

Tractors don't just pull things. They can lift, too. Tractors move bales around with a lifting arm on the front.

# Load and lift

**Tractors can do many jobs with lifting arms. They can load, grab or lift.**

## Loader

The lifting arms are called the **loader**. The driver controls the loader with electrical switches in the cab. Different attachments are put on to the front for different jobs.

Bucket

A bucket can scoop up rubble, gravel and dirt and tip it elsewhere.

**Grappler**

A grappler is like a claw. It picks a load up by grabbing it.

Prongs can also be fitted to the loader for lifting loads.

**Prongs**

# Pulling machines

**Tractors are not just found on farms. Their pulling power makes them useful in other places.**

## Breakdown rescue

Tractors can rescue vehicles that have broken down. These two tractors are pulling a truck that is trapped in a flood.

# Sea tractor

This tractor with caterpillar tracks pulls lifeboats into and out of the sea. It has been built to work in very deep water.

**Caterpillar tracks**

# Pulling contests

Tractor pulling has been made into a thrilling sport. Drivers of each tractor try to pull a heavy sled as far as they can. The power and weight can lift the tractor's front wheels off the ground!

# Tractors of old

**Tractors did not exist hundreds of years ago. So how did farmers do their work? They used horses to pull ploughs, harrows and seed drills.**

Horses wore heavy harnesses and were chained to the plough. Animals, such as horses and oxen, are still used on farms in parts of the world today.

**Harness**

By the 1800s, engines powered by steam were used on farms. The engines burnt coal to heat water and produce steam.

**Steam tractor**

In the 1920s petrol-powered tractors took over. Today, tractors use **diesel** fuel.

## Tractor fact

**One modern tractor can do the same work in a day as 200 horses!**

**1955**

# Monster tractors

All tractors are big, but some are absolute monsters. The biggest tractors must spread their weight with extra wheels. This stops the wheels churning up the land.

Other large tractors have caterpillar tracks (right).

Some tractors are so big that they bend in the middle to help them move around corners.

# Big Bud

***Big Bud* is the name of the world's largest tractor. Its fuel tank can hold over 3,700 litres of diesel!**

**Exhaust pipe:** This takes fumes away from the engine and carries them out into the air.

# Glossary

**caterpillar tracks**  metal bands that wrap around the wheels of a vehicle, for travel on rough ground

**combine harvester**  a huge machine which cuts and harvests crops, such as wheat and barley

**diesel**  a fuel burnt in tractor engines

**fertiliser**  a chemical added to the soil to make crops grow better

**harrow**  a heavy frame with spikes and discs, pulled over a ploughed field to break up the soil into fine pieces

**harvest**  gather crops once they have grown

**hay**  grass that is dried out and fed to animals

**hitch**  the links at the back of a tractor where machinery is attached

**horsepower**  a unit for measuring the power of an engine

**loader**  the two arms on the front of the tractor that can be attached with a part, such as a bucket, for lifting and carrying loads

**manure**  animal dung put on to the land to make crops grow better

**plough** turn over and cut the earth using a piece of farm equipment called a plough

**root vegetables** vegetables that grow under the ground

**seed drill** a device for sowing seeds into the earth

**shaft** a rotating bar that carries power from the engine to somewhere else

**vineyard** an area of farmland where grapes are grown

**weedkiller** a chemical sprayed on the land to destroy weeds

# Index

## Websites

**www.tractorland.co.uk/tractorland-fun.aspx**
This site has video clips of tractors in action.

**www.williamsbigbud.com/bigbud.htm**
Home of the world's largest tractor.

**www.challengermarketplace.com/public/images.php**
Look at the pictures in this fantastic tractor gallery.